HAVE THE FUNERAL
James MacDonald

Small-Group Experience written by
Neil Wilson

Have the Funeral
Small-Group Study Guide
Published by LifeWay Press®
©2011 James MacDonald
Reprinted December 2011

ISBN: 978-1-4158-6988-8
Item 005371572

Dewey Decimal Classification: 241.4
Subject Heading: FORGIVENESS \ HUMAN RELATIONS \ CHRISTIAN LIFE

Scripture quotations are from The Holy Bible, English Standard Version® (ESV®), copyright © 2001 by Crossway, a publishing ministry of Good News Publishers. Used by permission. All rights reserved.

To order additional copies of this resource, order online at *www.lifeway.com;* write LifeWay Small Groups; One LifeWay Plaza; Nashville, TN 37234-0175; fax order to (615) 251-5933; or call toll-free (800) 458-2772.

Printed in the United States of America

Leadership and Adult Publishing
LifeWay Church Resources
One LifeWay Plaza
Nashville, TN 37234-0175

ABOUT THIS STUDY

Welcome to *Have the Funeral*—a small-group Bible study from the *Platform* series. In this small-group experience, best-selling author and pastor James MacDonald helps us come to grips with the matter of forgiveness and what has to happen before we can practice this necessary spiritual discipline.

Here are the elements you'll be encountering during this small-group experience:

- **Warm-Up** – a time for sharing stories
- **Video Set-Up** – establishes context for your small-group time
- **Viewer Guide** – integral points from the video message to enhance discussion
- **Biblical Background** – biblical insight for greater understanding
- **Scripture** – all primary Scriptures are printed in the study guide
- **Small-Group Questions** – application, self-revelation, interpretation, or observation (discovery Bible study method builds community, invites God in, and generates transformational discussion)
- **Journal** – contributes to personal devotional time
- **You're Up** – a challenge for group members to practice what they have learned
- **Leader Notes** - in colored text at the beginning of each section

Leader: See pages 92-93 for details on how to create a memorable time of commitment for your members at the end of this experience.

Grieve and Leave

If you are a typical person, you are arriving at this study with a load. You are carrying the wounds and weight of accumulated offenses in your life. You've done your share of hurting others, but you certainly feel the sting of injuries that others have inflicted on you. There's part of you, maybe a huge part, that wants to be done with all that! You're tired of lugging all that baggage around. But you may wonder if there's a way you can forgive that is more than just lip service or a momentary, emotional release.

We're about to journey together to discover the crisis and the process of real forgiveness. If you will put into practice what you learn in the next six sessions, your life will be measurably different. Don't miss this golden opportunity to Have the Funeral.

WARM UP

Even in this do-it-yourself world, most of us know that there are some jobs that require an expert. It's nice to be known as a jack of all trades, but sooner or later, we run into situations where we don't know jack! What are some examples (they can be funny) of when you discovered and appreciated the necessity of having an expert do the job?

Let's begin by brainstorming a good definition of the word "forgiveness." James will give us his definition in a few moments, but let's talk about the kind of understanding of forgiveness we are bringing to the table at the start of this study.

VIDEO SET UP

The information below sets up the video. It can be read aloud to the group, read by group members ahead of time, or group members can read the information silently while the facilitator sets up the video.

In the video you are about to see, Pastor James will be standing in front of a casket. He is going to walk us through that sequence many of us have experienced as we've entered adulthood. Funerals can feel confusing or even creepy when we're children. As teenagers, we begin to feel that sense of loss and finality that comes when someone we know dies.

The crisis and process of forgiveness, James will tell us, is a lot like the necessary finality of a funeral. It has both the grieving and the leaving. We will see that both of these factors are significant when it comes to authentic forgiveness.

James wants to challenge us to have a crisis of forgiveness— an intentional time during which we focus entirely on the necessity of forgiveness: who we need to forgive, what we need to forgive, and the cost involved in forgiveness. Note in particular that although not the *means* of our salvation, forgiveness is essential as *evidence* of our salvation.

Take a moment to read the Scripture passages on page 12 before watching "Grieve and Leave" (13:23). Then discuss the two questions designed as follow-up to the video on the Viewer Guide page.

SHOW VIDEO NOW.

VIEWER GUIDE

Included are two questions designed as follow-up to "Grieve and Leave." This time is set aside for discussion within the group about what they heard, how it affected them, and possible applications. These questions may be only a beginning. Feel free to begin the conversation by asking what thoughts, insights, or stories had the most impact on group members.

1. How do you feel about James' definition of forgiveness ("the decision to release a person from the obligation that resulted when they injured you") given the earlier discussion about our understanding of forgiveness?

2. In what ways did James apply John 13:17 ("If you know these things, blessed are you if you do them") to forgiveness? Why do you think this might be a useful verse to memorize?

BIBLICAL BACKGROUND

With music there is usually a story behind the song that helps listeners appreciate the heart and soul behind both the music and the lyrics. Scripture is no different. Below you'll find a brief story behind this week's Scripture intended to provide additional understanding and insight.

As the unique God-Man, Jesus had a perspective on forgiveness that could only be grasped by those who believed in Him. He not only taught forgiveness, as we will see in Matthew 18, but He also demonstrated forgiveness. When this exchange with Peter occurred shortly after Jesus' transfiguration, the disciples had already witnessed Jesus exercising forgiveness with the paralytic man who had been lowered through the roof while Jesus was speaking to a packed house (Matthew 9:2-6). Jesus deliberately looked past the man's physical needs and addressed his deeper, spiritual needs, to the amazement of the crowd. He then proved His capacity and authority to forgive the man's sins by physically healing him.

Jesus forgave people who had sinned against Him as God, such as the woman caught in adultery (John 8:3-11), the woman who anointed His feet with oil (Luke 7:37-50), and even the believing criminal on the cross (Luke 23:39-43). But He also forgave those who rejected Him at the human level, asking His Father to forgive those who nailed Him to the cross (Luke 23:34). Jesus knew a lot about forgiveness and He practiced it in ways that are certain to give us hope.

SCRIPTURE

---

[17] **If you know these things, blessed are you if you do them.**
– John 13:17

[25] **And whenever you stand praying, forgive, if you have anything against anyone, so that your Father also who is in heaven may forgive you your trespasses.** – Mark 11:25

[37] **Judge not, and you will not be judged; condemn not, and you will not be condemned; forgive, and you will be forgiven.** – Luke 6:37

[9] **Pray then like this:**
"Our Father in heaven,
hallowed be your name.
[10] **Your kingdom come,**
>   **your will be done,**
>   **on earth as it is in heaven.**
[11] **Give us this day our daily bread,**
[12] **and forgive us our debts,**
>   **as we also have forgiven our debtors.**
– Matthew 6:9-12

For judgment is without mercy to one who has shown no mercy. Mercy triumphs over judgment. – James 2:13

SMALL-GROUP QUESTIONS

Over the next few pages you'll find discussion questions, material that may be used as additional discussion points, and a journal exercise for group members to complete away from the group.

"I want to challenge you this week to have a memorable crisis where you make the choice to forgive everyone who has ever done anything to injure you."

1. James talked about the significance of "grieve it and then leave it," not only in the loss caused by death but also in the loss caused by offenses and forgiveness. What did you take from those comments? How do you think those two things—death and forgiveness—are similar?

2. What risk did James take in admitting that he has a lot of firsthand experience in the process of forgiveness, and that it hasn't been easy for him? Does his admission heighten or lower his credibility for you as a teacher on this subject? What are the implications for you as you look to forgive?

ON THE SIDE

A young couple, deeply in love, meets with their pastor to plan their wedding ceremony. They invest countless hours in the details of that special event. One of their unspoken assumptions is that the magic of that single day will translate into the happily ever after of the marriage. It isn't easy to face reality before marriage, but the notion of happily ever after is often shattered when the honeymoon ends and life has its way.

The couple's pastor wants to give them a fighting chance. He's seen the truth in one of James' insights: "There are no lasting relationships without forgiveness."

So he takes this couple to the very place where they will exchange their wedding vows. The three of them go through the vows line by line so the couple can explain to one another what they will mean when they say those words during the wedding. It comes as quite a shock to them that they aren't really sure what they mean by "to have and to hold" or "to love and to cherish" (How are those things different?). They giggle over "for richer, for poorer," and then admit that their basic plan doesn't have room for "sickness," only "health." And they openly wonder if "for better, for worse" is bad luck for the marriage rather than a healthy view of the realities of life.

This couple won't be ready to talk about the necessity of forgiveness until they begin to grasp the fact that opportunities to forgive will absolutely come along.

"Forgiving people is not the means to God's forgiveness. It's not the plan of salvation. It's the proof of salvation."

3. Why do you think it was important for James to make this distinction between "plan" and "proof"?

4. How does James' discussion of the line from the Model Prayer ("Forgive us our debts as we forgive our debtors") affect your willingness to utter that prayer?

5. If forgiveness is "the proof of salvation," then why do you think some Christians say they are unwilling or unable to forgive? What are your reasons for not forgiving?

FIRSTHAND

If forgiveness is a combination of crisis and process, then the order is probably important for me to remember. It's tempting to dabble in the process first rather than face the crisis. The crisis is a doorway; the process is a journey. The crisis is a turning point; the process is a series of ongoing decisions. The crisis is intense, do or not do, final, and definite; the process involves time, includes backwards and forwards, growing, learning, and changing. A genuine crisis is not reversible while a process may include a certain amount of failure along the way.

Forgiveness is very much like being born. There's a lot of uncomfortable pressure, pain, and uncertainty in the moments of birth. Wouldn't it make more sense to skip the birth and get on with the living? No. Just as being born makes living possible, the crisis of forgiving makes the process of forgiveness possible. Trying the process of forgiveness without the crisis of forgiveness doesn't result in freedom.

"Forgiven people forgive."

James makes the point that in the life of a truly forgiven person, unforgiveness cannot long exist. The lack of resolution creates such misery in the heart of a forgiven person, such turmoil, that he has to forgive. Mark 11:25 says, "And whenever you stand praying, forgive, if you have anything against anyone, so that your Father also who is in heaven may forgive you your trespasses."

6. What do you think happens to our capacity to experience forgiveness when we insist that there are certain people and actions we can't forgive?

JOURNAL

This journaling opportunity is designed for group members to utilize at another time. They may choose to answer the question in the space provided or they may prefer to use the space and time to take a deep question or concern to God.

When it comes to forgiveness, grieving is the beginning of the crisis. It's the moment described by Jesus in Mark 11:25 when you are standing before God and certain painful situations or certain people's names and faces begin to fill your thoughts. Handling those moments is what these sessions are all about.

Consider compiling two lists below, using initials or some other code to keep this private at this point. List one is PINTF (People I Need to Forgive) and list two is PICF (People I Can't Forgive). These lists will be crucial in later sessions.

YOU'RE UP

To put into practice the lessons from God's Word in this session, keep the following things in mind:

- Recognize that if forgiveness were easy, everyone would be doing it right away.

- Ask God to help you see yourself and what He longs for you to experience through these sessions and the lifelong process of forgiveness.

- Meditate on how you would prove the truth of the statement: "There are no lasting relationships without forgiveness."

- Memorize the following definition of forgiveness and make it a point to ask people this week for their definition. Share in appropriate ways some of what you are learning about forgiveness.

"Forgiveness is the decision to release a person from the obligation that resulted when they injured you."

In the next session we will be thinking about the unpayable debt and to what degree each of us is liable for it. To prepare for the lesson, take a few minutes to read Matthew 18:15-35.

Unpayable Debt

Certain harsh realities like bankruptcies and foreclosures have awakened many people to the lunacy of trying to finance a lifestyle with debt. As a nation, the ship still seems to be heading into the vortex of ever-deeper debt, but more and more people are waking up to the issue of financial responsibility and a healthier view of money.

This session follows Jesus as He takes the timeless truth about the danger of debt and uses it to teach a profound lesson about forgiveness. The need for forgiveness is like an ever-mounting debt between ourselves and God and ourselves and others. If we don't get the debt of unforgiveness settled, we are in danger of permanent bondage.

WARM UP

Try not to spend too much time here, but let everyone answer the warm-up questions. Getting group members involved early helps create the best small-group environment.

In the opening video, we learned a definition of forgiveness. Let's say it together (either from memory or as follows):

> **"Forgiveness is the decision to release a person from the obligation that resulted when they injured you."**

For those who might not have been with us last time, and for our own review, what lasting thoughts or lessons did you take away from Session 1?

VIDEO SET UP

The information below sets up the video. It can be read aloud to the group, read by group members ahead of time, or group members can read the information silently while the facilitator sets up the video.

When we left James standing before a casket last time, he was challenging us with the concept that forgiven people forgive. We had some uncomfortable moments thinking about what we are inviting God to do each time we ask Him to "forgive us our debts as we also have forgiven our debtors" (Matthew 6:12). These convicting thoughts probably led to some reflection about our own struggles with forgiveness. In the Journal section it may have surprised us how many people immediately came to mind either as candidates for forgiveness or people we don't think we'll be able to forgive.

We begin this time with James addressing what happens when we don't forgive. James will help us look at some of the rationalizations that we use to justify not forgiving certain people. And we will be confronted with God's standard: we have to *always* forgive *everyone* for *everything*!

Take a moment to read the Scripture passages on pages 26-27 before watching "Unpayable Debt" (16:58). Then discuss the two questions designed as follow-up to the video on the Viewer Guide page.

SHOW VIDEO NOW.

VIEWER GUIDE

Included are two questions designed as follow-up to "Unpayable Debt."
This time is set aside for discussion within the group about what they heard,
how it affected them, and possible applications. These questions may
be only a beginning. Feel free to begin the conversation by asking what
thoughts, insights, or stories had the most impact on group members.

1. Let's start with what we just heard. Which one of those
   rationalizations are you most likely to use? Here they
   are again:

   a. The offense is too big.
   b. Time will heal it on its own.
   c. I'm waiting until they say they're sorry.
   d. I can't forgive what I can't forget.
   e. If I forgive, they will just do it again.

2. Which rationalization(s) did the unforgiving servant in
   Jesus' parable apply to his fellow servant? What did that
   reveal about his internalizing of the experience he had
   just had with his master? Have you experienced anything
   similar? Explain.

BIBLICAL BACKGROUND

With music there is usually a story behind the song that helps listeners appreciate the heart and soul behind both the music and the lyrics. Scripture is no different. Below you'll find a brief story behind this week's Scripture intended to provide additional understanding and insight.

Matthew, the tax-collector-turned-disciple, must have found the details of this parable fascinating from the perspective of his own life before he met Christ. The story was triggered by a question Peter asked: "Lord, how often will my brother sin against me, and I forgive him? As many as seven times?" (Matthew 18:21). Jesus proceeded to show how the citizens of God's kingdom act in ways that are quite opposite of the world's ways.

Jesus showed His disciples a truth that we can apply almost every day: common sense is also fallen sense. Sin infects every relationship, every decision, and every effort we make. We are never far from playing the role of the unforgiving servant. If our continual purpose is not to honor the One who forgave our unpayable debt, we will gradually slip back into living by the rules of the world rather than by the freedom of God's kingdom.

Peter thought he got the message, but he unwittingly tried to bring an "adjusted" rule into the kingdom by presenting himself as a "forgiveness machine" (offering seven-fold forgiveness). But Jesus showed Peter he wasn't even in the same time zone as the standard of the kingdom, which makes trying to keep a count of forgiveness a waste of time.

SCRIPTURE

²¹ Then Peter came up and said to him, "Lord, how often will my brother sin against me, and I forgive him? As many as seven times?"

²² Jesus said to him, "I do not say to you seven times, but seventy times seven. ²³ "Therefore the kingdom of heaven may be compared to a king who wished to settle accounts with his servants. ²⁴ When he began to settle, one was brought to him who owed him ten thousand talents. ²⁵ And since he could not pay, his master ordered him to be sold, with his wife and children and all that he had, and payment to be made.

²⁶ So the servant fell on his knees, imploring him, 'Have patience with me, and I will pay you everything.' ²⁷ And out of pity for him, the master of that servant released him and forgave him the debt.

^{28} But when that same servant went out, he found one of his fellow servants who owed him a hundred denarii, and seizing him, he began to choke him, saying, 'Pay what you owe.'
^{29} So his fellow servant fell down and pleaded with him, 'Have patience with me, and I will pay you.' ^{30} He refused and went and put him in prison until he should pay the debt.
^{31} When his fellow servants saw what had taken place, they were greatly distressed, and they went and reported to their master all that had taken place.
^{32} Then his master summoned him and said to him, 'You wicked servant! I forgave you all that debt because you pleaded with me. ^{33} And should not you have had mercy on your fellow servant, as I had mercy on you?' ^{34} And in anger his master delivered him to the jailers, until he should pay all his debt. ^{35} So also my heavenly Father will do to every one of you, if you do not forgive your brother from your heart."
– Matthew 18:21-35

SMALL-GROUP QUESTIONS

Over the next few pages you'll find discussion questions, material that may be used as additional discussion points, and a journal exercise for group members to complete away from the group.

1. Like most parables, Jesus' story of the unforgiving servant has a devastating application. What is it? To what is Matthew 18:35 referring?

"We *always* have to forgive *everyone* for *everything*! There is no limit."

2. What do you think it is that holds us back from agreeing wholeheartedly with the above statement? Which word gives you the most hesitation?

3. What sense do you get that James understands that he is asking some people to forgive others for unspeakable acts of evil?

4. Share with the group one of the things that you often struggle to forgive. What part of your story do you think makes this so difficult?

ON THE SIDE

One of the great stories of forgiveness in history is the shocking betrayal of young Joseph by his brothers and the way that offense played out over a lifetime (Genesis 37–50). Joseph was still a teenager when his older brothers let sibling jealousy get out of hand. They almost killed Joseph outright, but at the last minute decided to sell him into slavery, which they concluded was the same as killing him but without all the mess.

In spite of his brothers' actions, Joseph survived and even thrived. But he also experienced some crushing setbacks. After significantly increasing the prosperity of his owner in Egypt, Joseph was sexually harassed by the man's wife and accused of rape. Sent to prison unjustly, he again made the best of the situation and, as a result of unusual circumstances, ended up as the second in charge of Egypt, trusted to help a nation survive a horrific famine. All of this eventually brought Joseph's brothers back into his life, but this time they were completely dependent on him for their survival. And they had no idea this powerful man was their long-gone little brother.

In the amazing events that follow, we can't know for sure what Joseph was thinking, but it's clear that he had forgiven his brothers. We can't know when Joseph made the choice to forgive. Was it as the slave traders dragged him off into the desert? Was it when he realized God had brought his family back into his life? The life Joseph led as a slave indicates that he had already developed a strong relationship with God which included being able to see that even his brothers' betrayal was something God could use.

Years later, when Jacob died, the brothers revealed they still felt a lot of guilt about how they treated Joseph and even suspected he might have been waiting to take revenge until their father died. This led to a remarkable exchange:

[16] So they sent a message to Joseph, saying, "Your father gave this command before he died, [17] 'Say to Joseph, Please forgive the transgression of your brothers and their sin, because they did evil to you.' And now, please forgive the transgression of the servants of the God of your father." Joseph wept when they spoke to him. [18] His brothers also came and fell down before him and said, "Behold, we are your servants." [19] But Joseph said to them, "Do not fear, for am I in the place of God? [20] As for you, you meant evil against me, but God meant it for good, to bring it about that many people should be kept alive, as they are today."
– Genesis 50:16-20

5. As you look over the list of five major rationalizations, what makes each of them inadequate?

   a. The offense is too big.
   b. Time will heal it on its own.
   c. I'm waiting until they say they're sorry.
   d. I can't forgive what I can't forget.
   e. If I forgive, they will just do it again.

JOURNAL

This journaling opportunity is designed for group members to utilize at another time. They may choose to answer the questions in the space provided or they may prefer to use the space and time to take a deep question or concern to God.

Review the two lists you began in last week's journaling segment. Do any names need to be moved from one list to another?

Now that you are considering this lesson on your own, which of those rationalizations do you need to disown? Ask God to help you toward a crisis of forgiveness.

YOU'RE UP

As you participate in the crisis and process of forgiveness this week, keep the following questions in mind:

- At what point, if ever, did you recognize you were born with an unpayable debt to God, making you spiritually bankrupt? What did you do about that realization?

- If you consider yourself completely forgiven by God, what would keep Him from being able to say to you as He said to the unforgiving servant, "You wicked servant! I forgave you all that debt because you pleaded with me. And should not you have had mercy on your fellow servant, as I had mercy on you?" (Matthew 18:32-33).

- What do you fear would happen if you did forgive the people on your lists?

- Ask God to give you the courage to grieve and to leave.

In the next session we will look at some of the fallout that happens when we don't forgive. If we can step back for a moment, with God's help, from the hurts that draw our attention, we may be able to see more clearly that we have good and compelling reasons to forgive.

The Human Element

Are you tired? Do you find that exhaustion is a constant undercurrent in your life? What kind of work are you doing that makes you so tired? One of the overlooked reasons why unforgiveness is so devastating is that it takes huge amounts of energy to keep it raging. The offenses have to be reviewed and measured for added items to add to the list of hurts. Like an energy-sapping program running in the background of our life-computer, unforgiveness uses up God's gifts that could be much better employed in other areas of life. Forgiveness is energizing; unforgiveness drains our emotional batteries dry.

WARM UP

Try not to spend too much time here, but let everyone answer the warm-up questions. Getting group members involved early helps create the best small-group environment.

Here's a fun little English exercise. Let's all try to come up with a sentence that uses the term "fallout" correctly. And I don't mean "I put on my seat belt so I don't *fall out* of the car." Any ideas?

What have you found most memorable about Sessions 1 and 2?

VIDEO SET UP

The information below sets up the video. It can be read aloud to the group, read by group members ahead of time, or group members can read the information silently while the facilitator sets up the video.

This session presents a warning and encouragement about forgiveness by spelling out the kind of long-term and often invisible fallout that is generated by unforgiveness. The effects can damage us physically, developmentally, psychologically, and ultimately spiritually. We can certainly identify some of these effects in the parable of the unforgiving servant, but we can also spot them in our own lives.

In the previous two sessions, the focus has been on the interpersonal, or external, issues that keep us from embracing forgiveness. In this session we will see that there are huge intrapersonal, or internal, reasons to forgive early and often.

Once motivated, we will still need God's enabling to undergo the crisis and the process of forgiveness. An important shift is going to take place during the crisis of forgiveness that moves the responsibility from the perpetrator to the victim. The relationship priority for a person in the process of forgiveness is no longer primarily with the person who caused the hurt but rather with God who is now actively involved in healing.

Take a moment to read the Scriptures on pages 40-41 before watching "The Human Element" (16:49). Then discuss the questions designed as follow-up to the video on the Viewer Guide page.

SHOW VIDEO NOW.

VIEWER GUIDE

Included are two questions designed as follow-up to "The Human Element." This time is set aside for discussion within the group about what they heard, how it affected them, and possible applications. These questions may be only a beginning. Feel free to begin the conversation by asking what thoughts, insights, or stories had the most impact on group members.

1. What does James mean when he says, "The fallout of unforgiveness is huge!" How has this proven true in your own life?

2. What are the three "I won't bring it up" statements that are central to the process of forgiveness, and what does each one mean?

BIBLICAL BACKGROUND

With music there is usually a story behind the song that helps listeners appreciate the heart and soul behind both the music and the lyrics. Scripture is no different. Below you'll find a brief story behind this week's Scripture intended to provide additional understanding and insight.

Like many of Jesus' parables, the story of the unforgiving servant appeals to a universal desire for justice. We are struck by the mercy shown the first servant by his master in forgiving the un-payable debt. The servant didn't deserve to be let off the hook. When the master confronted him with the overwhelming debt, the servant was in denial. He begged, "Have patience with me, and I will pay you everything" (Matthew 18:26b). It seems he didn't even understand the weight of his debt, yet it was totally forgiven. Clearly, the reality of what had just happened to the servant didn't penetrate his heart because he, now a debt-free man, walked out still thinking he would somehow pay it back. He had not accepted the forgiveness offered.

No wonder the servant's next moves stun our sense of justice. When he attacks his fellow servant, we feel outraged that he would do anything other than pay forward the amazing gift just given to him. We don't feel badly when, a few verses later, the master reimposes the debt on the first servant. In that moment of felt justice, Jesus turns to us and says, "So also my heavenly Father will do to every one of you, if you do not forgive your brother from your heart" (Matthew 18:35).

As we read Jesus' concluding words, we are like the Old Testament King David who, caught in the crosshairs of Nathan's parable, suddenly realized he had pulled the trigger of truth aimed at himself (2 Samuel 12:1-14). Our heightened sense of justice gets applied painfully to us. We thought Jesus was telling an interesting story about fairness and forgiveness, but now we realize that He was telling a story about us. And the truth of that story requires a response.

SCRIPTURE

---

[14] For if you forgive others their trespasses, your heavenly Father will also forgive you. – Matthew 6:14

[28] But when that same servant went out, he found one of his fellow servants who owed him a hundred denarii, and seizing him, he began to choke him, saying, "Pay what you owe." [29] So his fellow servant fell down and pleaded with him, "Have patience with me, and I will pay you."

[30] He refused and went and put him in prison until he should pay the debt. [31] When his fellow servants saw what had taken place, they were greatly distressed, and they went and reported to their master all that had taken place.

^{32} Then his master summoned him and said to him, "You wicked servant! I forgave you all that debt because you pleaded with me. ^{33} And should not you have had mercy on your fellow servant, as I had mercy on you?" ^{34} And in anger his master delivered him to the jailers, until he should pay all his debt. ^{35} So also my heavenly Father will do to every one of you, if you do not forgive your brother from your heart. – Matthew 8:28-35

^{1} And he said to his disciples, "Temptations to sin are sure to come, but woe to the one through whom they come! ^{2} It would be better for him if a millstone were hung around his neck and he were cast into the sea than that he should cause one of these little ones to sin. ^{3} Pay attention to yourselves! If your brother sins, rebuke him, and if he repents, forgive him, ^{4} and if he sins against you seven times in the day, and turns to you seven times, saying, 'I repent,' you must forgive him." – Luke 17:1-4

SMALL-GROUP QUESTIONS

Over the next few pages you'll find discussion questions, material that may be used as additional discussion points, and a journal exercise for group members to complete away from the group.

"Unforgiveness is a punisher. But it doesn't punish the person who sinned; unforgiveness punishes the person who was sinned against."

1. What does the statement above mean? Isn't the point of unforgiveness to hold out for some kind of retribution or payback for the offense?

2. In one sense, unforgiveness seems so focused—one offender acutely in mind. So, how does James liken holding on to an offense to a tornado randomly tearing up someone's life?

3. Unforgiveness is a condition rather than a feeling. What emotions do you associate most closely with unforgiveness? Why?

ON THE SIDE

Steve Saint sat around a fire late into the night, sharing stories with the older men of the Waodani tribe in Ecuador. Everyone in that circle shared a common bond in Jesus Christ. They also shared almost half a century of history that had begun with a terrible tragedy when five missionaries, including Steve's father Nate, had been killed by the same men whose company he now enjoyed. That night Steve learned something he didn't know about Mincaye, a Waodani warrior who had become his adopted father in the years that the gospel and the New Testament in Waodani had changed the world of that tribe. Mincaye, now a minister of the gospel himself, had even baptized some of Steve's children.

As the men spoke in hushed tones once again about the tragic events on "Palm Beach," Mincaye told Steve that he had delivered the blow that had killed Steve's father. This wasn't a confession; it was simply a detail that had never been told. As Steve looked at the face of his father's killer reflected in the firelight, he realized the news didn't matter. What mattered was everything that God had accomplished in thousands of lives altered in part by the death of five of His servants.

Steve has been asked many times about the struggles he must have had to forgive those who took his father from him. He has always said that it was never a struggle for him. Even alongside his childhood grief, he somehow realized that his father's death had been part of God's plan.

4. In what different ways can we see that the first servant in Jesus' parable never actually received the forgiveness that was offered him? As James put it, "it never penetrated his heart."

"When God says 'Don't,' He means 'Don't hurt yourself.'"

5. Have you seen people who are *not* directly involved in a situation get hurt deeply by the fallout of unforgiveness? In what ways?

FIRSTHAND

At the close of the video segment for Session 3, James refers to the personal cost of forgiveness. There is a debt or payment required in forgiveness and the one who pays it is the one who forgives. The victim "funds" forgiveness.

When my child shatters a family heirloom, I'm faced with numerous challenges. The heirloom may be irreplaceable. The breakage may have been an accident or careless disobedience of my rule not to kick the soccer ball in the house. There may have to be discipline/punishment for deliberate disobedience. And if the broken item can be replaced, there may have to be some arrangement for restitution. And I will need to forgive my child. Parent-child relationships are forgiveness laboratories!

Even after the above occurs, the heirloom will remain shattered. Even if the item is replaced, it will not be the same treasured one. The "payment" to accept the altered state of things is born by the one who forgives. This helps me understand the "payment" aspect of God's forgiveness. Colossians 2:13-14 says, "And you, who were dead in your trespasses and the uncircumcision of your flesh, God made alive together with him, having forgiven us all our trespasses, by canceling the record of debt that stood against us with its legal demands. This he set aside, nailing it to the cross." If we stop with the "canceling" part, we will miss the "nailing it to the cross" part. The debt the Bible speaks about doesn't involve a third party that God pays on our behalf. The "debt" was our offense against a holy God that only a holy God could resolve. What was impossible to repair or replace, God being God was able to repair and replace at an incredible cost to Himself. God does the impossible (see Mark 10:27).

6. Discuss the dangers revealed by James' statement, "If you esteem what you've experienced as greater injury than our sin in the eyes of a holy God, then you don't understand your true condition."

7. Explain why forgiveness is *not* the following:

- Enabling – Supplying the means for repeated behavior

- Rescuing – Shielding someone from the consequences of their own decisions
- Risking – Ignoring a pattern of abuse

JOURNAL

This journaling opportunity is designed for group members to utilize at another time. They may choose to answer the question in the space provided or they may prefer to use the space and time to take a deep question or concern to God.

At this point in the crisis or process of forgiveness, how are you doing with the two lists you began in Session 1? What would you say it's going to take to move every name on the "People I Can't Forgive" list to the "People I Need to Forgive" list? What are you risking between you and God with every name you leave on the "Can't" list?

YOU'RE UP

While you consider God's role and will in your life, consider these first steps:

- Ask God to help you see yourself as He sees you, with every one of your offenses nailed to the cross of Jesus.

- Clarify in the particular situations you face what forgiveness will *not* mean or require. Ask someone you trust to verify that you are not continuing a self-destructive pattern under the guise of "I've forgiven, but won't _____."

- Track what happens in the cases where you have already gone through the crisis of forgiveness and are now practicing the three "won't bring it up" rules (to them, to others, to myself). What difference does this process make?

- Ask God to bring you to the crisis you need in order to accept His supernatural help to do the impossible and genuinely forgive every person on both of your lists.

Next week we will look at just what it will take to begin the next steps in the journey of forgiveness. We come face to face with how our lack of forgiveness becomes an offense to a holy God.

Prepare for Burial

Our perception that something is going to be very hard to do sometimes makes doing it even harder than it needs to be. We avoid the crisis of forgiveness because we think it will be too hard, only to discover later that it was actually harder to keep holding on to unforgiveness! A toothache won't go away because we are afraid of the dentist. Sliding into the "chair" of forgiveness may not be easy, but the relief after the process of drilling and filling will be worth the crisis of submitting to the pain. Unforgiveness causes cavities in our lives. So let's start by making an appointment with God.

WARM UP

Try not to spend too much time here, but let everyone answer the warm-up questions. Getting group members involved early helps create the best small-group environment. If you haven't done so yet, have everyone take a look at the card (p. 93) they will be filling out for the burial at the conclusion of this study.

Let's take a few minutes and celebrate together the amazing gift of decision-making that God has given us. What are some of the earliest memories you have of realizing you could make a choice and act on it? How did that realization affect you?

What is one significant insight about forgiveness you have learned from the first three sessions of this study?

VIDEO SET UP

The information below sets up the video. It can be read aloud to the group, read by group members ahead of time, or group members can read the information silently while the facilitator sets up the video.

In case we haven't "gotten it" yet, in this session we get an unavoidable confrontation with God's expectations about our practice of forgiveness. We are sometimes so overwhelmed and hurt by the offenses against us that we fail to recognize that holding on to those offenses becomes an offense to God.

We may think we are practicing holiness by maintaining a high standard of what we call justice, but actually we are being drawn into a self-destructive pattern of unforgiveness. If you haven't had a crisis of forgiveness yet, when you start thinking of what is involved in total, immediate, unilateral forgiveness, that crisis will quickly develop.

At times it seems easier to hold on to unforgiveness. It seems so right! Our injured soul may silently shout, "It's my right to hold this!" But God says, "Don't," and as we learned last time, when God says "Don't," what He means is "Don't hurt yourself."

Take a moment to read the Scripture passages on pages 54-55 before watching "Prepare for Burial" (12:34). Then discuss the two questions designed as follow-up to the video on the Viewer Guide page.

SHOW VIDEO NOW.

VIEWER GUIDE

Included are two questions designed as follow-up to "Prepare for Burial." This time is set aside for discussion within the group about what they heard, how it affected them, and possible applications. These questions may be only a beginning. Feel free to begin the conversation by asking what thoughts, insights, or stories had the most impact on group members.

1. What part of total, immediate, unilateral forgiveness do you think is hardest for people to consider seriously?

2. How did you respond to James' description of "training your mind to think differently" in this video presentation? Where are you in this journey?

BIBLICAL BACKGROUND

With music there is usually a story behind the song that helps listeners appreciate the heart and soul behind both the music and the lyrics. Scripture is no different. Below you'll find a brief story behind this week's Scripture intended to provide additional understanding and insight.

As with each of his letters, the apostle Paul used a teach/apply approach to his communication with the Ephesian Christians. The first half of his letter (chs. 1–3) primarily establishes who we are and what we have in Christ. Those three chapters present a concentrated dose of theology—the big picture between God and us. Chapters 4–6 are the extremely practical results that should occur if we take the first three chapters seriously. Chapter 4 begins with "I therefore" (v. 1), stating Paul's transition from "this is what you need to know" to "this is what you need to do."

Twenty-five verses into chapter four, Paul comes back to "therefore." In the preceding verses (17-24), he developed a couple of pictures of life that can help us understand God's practical concerns. The same crisis/process sequence that we have been considering regarding forgiveness is applied to all of life. The crisis of conversion/salvation leads to the process of sanctification/discipleship. Paul tells us the process is a lot like taking off old, soiled clothes (v. 22), experiencing a change of thinking patterns (v. 23), and then putting on the clothing of a new self, marked by holiness and righteousness (v. 24).

After giving us the big picture, Paul fills us in on the details. The old clothes are falsehood (v. 25), anger (v. 26), and stealing (v. 28), and the new, clean clothes are truth (v. 25), not letting the sun go down on anger (v. 26), and honest work and sharing (v. 28). This brings us to the heart of the practical passage that we will focus on in this and the final two sessions.

SCRIPTURE

---

[25] Therefore, having put away falsehood, let each one of you speak the truth with his neighbor, for we are members one of another. [26] Be angry and do not sin; do not let the sun go down on your anger, [27] and give no opportunity to the devil. [28] Let the thief no longer steal, but rather let him labor, doing honest work with his own hands, so that he may have something to share with anyone in need. [29] Let no corrupting talk come out of your mouths, but only such as is good for building up, as fits the occasion, that it may give grace to those who hear. [30] And do not grieve the Holy Spirit of God, by whom you were sealed for the day of redemption. [31] Let all bitterness and wrath and anger and clamor and slander be put away from you, along with all malice. [32] Be kind to one another, tenderhearted, forgiving one another, as God in Christ forgave you. – Ephesians 4:25-32

[16] And I will ask the Father, and he will give you another Helper, to be with you forever, [17] even the Spirit of truth, whom the world cannot receive, because it neither sees him nor knows him. You know him, for he dwells with you and will be in you. – John 14:16-17

[13] In him you also, when you heard the word of truth, the gospel of your salvation, and believed in him, were sealed with the promised Holy Spirit, [14] who is the guarantee of our inheritance until we acquire possession of it, to the praise of his glory. – Ephesians 1:13-14

[5] For he has said, "I will never leave you nor forsake you." [6] So we can confidently say, "The Lord is my helper; I will not fear; what can man do to me?" – Hebrews 13:5b-6

SMALL-GROUP QUESTIONS

Over the next few pages you'll find discussion questions, material that may be used as additional discussion points, and a journal exercise for group members to complete away from the group.

> "When Jesus said, 'I'll never leave you or forsake you,' He was talking about the ministering presence of the Holy Spirit."

1. In Ephesians 4:30, we are told not to "grieve the Holy Spirit." How do you understand this statement? In what ways might you have been guilty of grieving the Spirit?

2. In Ephesians 1:13, Paul describes the process of salvation as including our being "sealed with the promised Holy Spirit." What does that mean to us in regard to forgiveness?

ON THE SIDE

If unforgiveness is mercilessly and completely self-destructive, then accepting God's standard for forgiveness is like a super power taking seriously a non-nuclear proliferation treaty. The Cold War depended on a principle called "mutual assured destruction" (M.A.D.) as the ultimate deterrent against one side pressing the nuclear launch button. The other side had enough weapons that they could retaliate even to a surprise attack so that the end result would not be victory but mutual devastation—the ultimate global lose-lose proposition.

Unforgiveness operates by a principle that seems like M.A.D., with the finger of anger, hurt, and vengeance poised over the button of retaliation. However, the actual situation could be described as S.A.D. (self-assured destruction), for while firmly holding on to our offenses and injuries may seem like the only viable plan for survival, it actually leads to our own destruction.

This is why total, immediate, unilateral forgiveness is not a treaty you establish with other people to avoid hurts, but rather a treaty you establish with yourself—with God as witness—as a way to deal with hurts that will inevitably come.

3. Expand on each of the terms used by James to define the parameters of forgiveness:

• Total -

• Immediate -

• Unilateral -

"Some people say you don't have to forgive a person until they repent. That is not correct."

4. What makes Luke 17:4 unique in the New Testament among the verses about forgiveness? "And if he sins against you seven times in the day, and turns to you seven times, saying, 'I repent,' you must forgive him." See also Matthew 6:12,14-15; 18:21-22; Mark 11:25.

"Don't inform someone you forgive them unless they repent—even though you have already forgiven them."

5.   How might announcing unsolicited forgiveness derail or devalue the offense?

6.   When Jesus forgave those who nailed Him to the cross, to whom was He speaking and why was that an unusual circumstance? (See Luke 23:34.) What does it teach us about forgiveness in our own lives?

FIRSTHAND

It is shockingly easy to take God's forgiveness for granted. This is the danger we face when we insist on holding on to our unforgiveness while at the same time claiming to enjoy God's forgiveness. We employ a verse like 1 John 1:9—"If we confess our sins, he is faithful and just to forgive us our sins and to cleanse us from all unrighteousness"—as if reading it out loud is the equivalent of confession and repentance. But genuine repentance demonstrates an understanding of the offense we have caused. And the offense toward God caused by our sin is always beyond our full understanding. If we do not develop an ever-expanding sense of where we would be if not for the grace of God's forgiveness, we will withhold forgiveness from others.

The fact is that we take God's forgiveness for granted much more than the forgiveness of others. This is why we seldom ask one another for forgiveness. The vulnerability required in order to admit wrongdoing and ask him or her to pardon us often keeps us from reconciliation. It also causes us to apologize rather than ask for forgiveness. "I'm sorry" is simply a declaration and it doesn't require any response from the other person. It is only an expression of how we feel; not a willingness to give the other person a choice to forgive or to retaliate.

In my relationship with God, the crisis of repentance that leads to salvation opens the way for an ongoing process of repentance.
In this process, I continue to learn the length, breadth, depth, and height of God's love and forgiveness by continually confessing my ongoing failures and sins. It is that immediacy of God's forgiveness that shapes my willingness to forgive others.

"To insist on carrying an offense is a sin and hinders your relationship with God."

7. How would you illustrate from your own experiences the truth of the statement above?

JOURNAL

This journaling opportunity is designed for group members to utilize at another time. They may choose to answer the questions in the space provided or they may prefer to use the space and time to take a deep question or concern to God.

While you are considering those people you must forgive, what kind of list could you compile of people from whom you need to ask forgiveness?

How does your need to be forgiven affect your willingness to forgive others?

YOU'RE UP

To live more fully in the life Christ came to give you, consider acting on these things:

- Train yourself to avoid the three danger zones: talking about the offense to the person, to others, and to yourself.

- Look at your forgiveness card (p. 93) at least once a day, asking God to help you make it as complete as possible, listing the people and the pain you choose to forgive.

- Ask God to give you a fresh awareness of the priceless gift of His forgiveness. Ask Him to help you learn to grieve over those things that grieve His Spirit.

- Be aware of the people the Holy Spirit brings to your mind as candidates you need to forgive or people from whom you need to ask forgiveness.

Next week we will look at what's in forgiveness for us that makes it worth the risk. What are the benefits of forgiveness?

May They Rest in Peace

When it comes to sports teams, most of us find it easier to trash talk the opposition than to extol the virtues of the team we support. If the other team's flaws aren't obvious, we can always make up a few that will justify our dislike. Unforgiveness requires advanced degrees in trash talking the people who hurt us. Our motto becomes: "How have you hurt me? Let me count the ways!" We can wax eloquent on the shortcomings, faults, and despicable traits of those who have hurt us. Our capacity for compassion and our ability to identify with the people who have offended us can be the first things to go as we descend into unforgiveness. Thankfully, we become healthier people when we practice forgiveness.

WARM UP

Try not to spend too much time here, but let everyone answer the warm-up questions. Getting group members involved early helps create the best small-group environment.

If we were going to compile a list of "things that are easy to forgive," what kinds of offenses would you add?

What are some recent examples of things for which you had to ask God for forgiveness?

VIDEO SET UP

The information below sets up the video. It can be read aloud to the group, read by group members ahead of time, or group members can read the information silently while the facilitator sets up the video.

In this session, James will walk us through the details of Ephesians 4:31-32. If we are determined not to grieve the Holy Spirit, who is our on-board connection with God, certain things must go and certain things must be put in place. As we discovered last time, we will have to undergo training at the mind level to think differently about life and about the people who injure us. We have already determined that the process of forgiveness means we don't talk about the issue to those who have hurt us; to others, or to ourselves. This time, James is going to point out the specific kinds of talking that goes on which not only grieves the Holy Spirit but also reveals lingering unforgiveness in us. These verses spell out six specific negative kinds of talk that must be eliminated from our approach to life if we are going to cultivate a habit of forgiveness.

Today's video begins by seeking to address the questions you might be thinking: *Why have the crisis? What's in forgiveness for me?* It turns out there are three highly beneficial reasons for extending forgiveness. This session we will focus on the first one: forgiveness eliminates damaging emotions.

Take a moment to read the Scriptures on page 70 before watching "May They Rest in Peace" (10:11). Then discuss the follow-up questions on the Viewer Guide page.

SHOW VIDEO NOW.

VIEWER GUIDE

Included are two questions designed as follow-up to "May They Rest in Peace." This time is set aside for discussion within the group about what they heard, how it affected them, and possible applications. These questions may be only a beginning. Feel free to begin the conversation by asking what thoughts, insights, or stories had the most impact on group members.

1. *Bitterness, wrath, anger, clamor, slander,* and *malice.* Which of these would you say you are most familiar with? Explain.

2. Why does James refer to these as "damaging emotions?" What kind of damage do they cause?

BIBLICAL BACKGROUND

With music there is usually a story behind the song that helps listeners appreciate the heart and soul behind both the music and the lyrics. Scripture is no different. Below you'll find a brief story behind this week's Scripture intended to provide additional understanding and insight.

Certain lists in Scripture appear to be random; others give evidence of intentional sequence. For example, the fruits of the Spirit listed in Galatians 5:22-23 are probably not sequential in the sense of the earlier being essential to the later ones. They can be apparent in a Christian's life in any order, and some may be more obvious at certain times as circumstances require.

The list Paul gives us in Ephesians 4:31, however, appears to be cumulative: "Let all bitterness and wrath and anger and clamor and slander be put away from you, along with all malice." It begins with bitterness, and each rung on the ladder of damaging emotions takes us lower until we reach malice. Each level of damaging emotions incorporates the ones before. Bitterness is almost entirely internal while the focus of malice is almost entirely external. We could actually call this list the fruits of unforgiveness, for each of those negative expressions can be traced back to offenses we have chosen not to forgive.

Understanding the sequence of negative emotions can help us identify the starting point of healing. We can ask for God's help in eliminating the step we're on and then stepping up until we are back at the top, leaving bitterness and its friends below.

SCRIPTURE

---

³¹ Let all bitterness and wrath and anger and clamor and slander be put away from you, along with all malice. ³² Be kind to one another, tenderhearted, forgiving one another, as God in Christ forgave you. – Ephesians 4:31-32

⁵ Put to death therefore what is earthly in you: sexual immorality, impurity, passion, evil desire, and covetousness, which is idolatry. ⁶ On account of these the wrath of God is coming. ⁷ In these you too once walked, when you were living in them. ⁸ But now you must put them all away: anger, wrath, malice, slander, and obscene talk from your mouth. ⁹ Do not lie to one another, seeing that you have put off the old self with its practices. – Colossians 3:5-9

¹⁵ See to it that no one fails to obtain the grace of God; that no "root of bitterness" springs up and causes trouble, and by it many become defiled. – Hebrews 12:15

SMALL-GROUP QUESTIONS

Over the next few pages you'll find discussion questions, material that may be used as additional discussion points, and a journal exercise for group members to complete away from the group.

1. How does hurt lead to unforgiveness, which then leads to bitterness, followed by the other damaging emotions? What's the process of unforgiveness that parallels the process of forgiveness?

"The bitter person looks at life like an umpire—always calling others out."

2. In what ways is bitterness like drinking poison but expecting the other person to die?

ON THE SIDE

One of the most amazing depictions of the downward spiral of damaging emotions can be found in the award-winning movie *Amadeus*, the story of the composer Mozart told through the eyes of a jealous competitor composer named Salieri. In this story, jealousy is compounded by hurt and unforgiveness, leading eventually to malice as Salieri seeks to destroy Mozart.

The music playing throughout this movie is a stunning example of God's gifts, which are bestowed in ways we don't often understand. In the end, Salieri destroys himself in an effort to surpass Mozart. His relationship with God is destroyed. He imagines he has used his own musical gifts to praise God but in the end his life is devoured in the feast of unforgiveness where the one who refuses to forgive is the main course.

3. What do you think wrath adds to bitterness?

"Anger is like a volcano: an outburst of rage, a violent explosion that dissipates quickly."

4. What makes anger such a damaging emotion in relationships? How is Ephesians 4:26-27 a helpful strategy?

5. How do "clamor" (the demand to have one's grievances heard), "slander" (the deliberate use of lies and distortions to harm another) and "malice" (an evil inclination toward others) represent the final steps in the downward spiral of unforgiveness? What does this kind of destruction look like in a person's life?

FIRSTHAND

There are now numerous sites online which allow people to process their efforts at forgiveness. A site called *theforgivenessproject.com* has compiled stories from around the world of people in the process of forgiveness. This is not necessarily a Christian site, but it demonstrates that the alternatives to forgiveness are worse than anything forgiveness requires of us.

We think forgiveness is hard, and it is. But we don't stop to think often enough about the cost of the alternatives: unforgiveness and revenge. These two reactions are certainly ways to respond to hurts of various kinds, but unfortunately they continue the cycle of pain given and received. Unforgiveness and revenge do not lead to health and healing; they lead to more of the same.

No wonder the cycle of bitterness to malice that Paul described is downward. The feelings intensify because the destruction is expanding. Unforgiveness is like a wild forest fire: it may start with a tiny spark of bitterness, but if left to run its course, it grows and destroys everything it its path.

"Don't confuse understandable with excusable."

6. What did James mean by his warning not to confuse the
    process of understanding our unforgiveness with excusing
    our unforgiveness? Using the forest fire analogy, what
    might it look like when a person chooses to forgive?

JOURNAL

This journaling opportunity is designed for group members to utilize at another time. They may choose to answer the question in the space provided or they may prefer to use the space and time to take a deep question or concern to God.

The plan for the final session involves embracing the crisis of forgiveness. The card you have been working on (p. 93) will need to be completed between now and the next time your group meets. What, if anything, do you think is holding you back from entering into total, immediate, unilateral forgiveness?

Ask God for the courage and the strength you need to finally and completely forgive *everything everyone* has *ever* done to you.

YOU'RE UP

As you participate in the crises and process of forgiveness this week, keep the following questions in mind:

- How many of the damaging emotions surveyed in this session are a familiar part of your life?

- Has anything positive come out of those emotions?

- What changes do you expect and/or fear will come about if you forgive the people who have hurt you?

- Ask God to help you see yourself as someone He has taught to forgive.

Next week we will follow through on our commitment to forgive. Make sure you bring your card so we can have the funeral!

Leave the Gravesite Behind

As hard as it is to think and pray seriously about forgiveness, it isn't the same as practicing forgiveness. No matter how long you walk along the cliff of forgiveness, wondering how difficult it will be to leave unforgiveness behind, the experience will be very different when you finally step over the edge. Forgiveness is not falling; it's flying! As long as you limp along the sad, hard, exhausting flats of unforgiveness, afraid you might fall off what seems like the bottomless cliff of forgiveness, you will never experience firsthand the lightness and freedom of flight. It's time, not just to face the crisis, but to run right through it!

WARM UP

Try not to spend too much time here, but let everyone answer the warm-up questions. Getting group members involved early helps create the best small-group environment.

What is the saddest movie you've ever seen? Did it move you to tears? If so, what part of your story do you think caused that reaction to the movie?

What does grieving mean to you? How do we know when grief is over?

VIDEO SET UP

The information below sets up the video. It can be read aloud to the group, read by group members ahead of time, or group members can read the information silently while the facilitator sets up the video.

The content of James' final presentation will include the other three of the four healthy alternatives to unforgiveness. Last time we discussed eliminating the downward spiral of negative emotions that spring from unforgiveness. This time we will see that in the process of forgiveness, healing efforts are renewed, healing attitudes are restored, and Christ's example is elevated.

The video leads us right into the crisis of turning in our forgiveness cards (p. 93), creating the memorable choice of releasing others from the obligation that resulted when they injured us. Releasing them means we are no longer tethered to them. We may have feared what would happen if we cut them free, but the main thing that will immediately happen is that we become free!

Take a moment to read the Scriptures on page 84 before watching "Leave the Gravesite Behind" (20:20). Then discuss the follow-up questions on the Viewer Guide page.

SHOW VIDEO NOW.

VIEWER GUIDE

Included are two questions designed as follow-up to "Leave the Gravesite Behind." This time is set aside for discussion within the group about what they heard, how it affected them, and possible applications. These questions may be only a beginning. Feel free to begin the conversation by asking what thoughts, insights, or stories had the most impact on group members.

1. What people come to mind when you think of the words "kind" and "tenderhearted"? How have these people influenced your life?

2. In what lasting relationships in your life have you discovered the truth that "there are no enduring relationships without forgiveness"?

BIBLICAL BACKGROUND

With music there is usually a story behind the song that helps listeners appreciate the heart and soul behind both the music and the lyrics. Scripture is no different. Below you'll find a brief story behind this week's Scripture intended to provide additional understanding and insight.

One of the limitations of English is the dual role that the word "you" has to carry in representing both the singular and plural meanings. In order to minimize confusion, sometimes "all" is added to make "you all," an expression that points to corporate solidarity. Paraphrasing this session's Scripture using this phrase would result in: "And do not grieve the Holy Spirit of God, by whom you all were sealed for the day of redemption. Let all bitterness and wrath and anger and clamor and slander be put away from you all, along with all malice. Be kind to one another, tenderhearted, forgiving one another, as God in Christ forgave you all" (Ephesians 4:30-32, paraphrase added).

We read these passages of Scripture as individuals, so we usually think of the "you" usages as singular, but they are almost always plural. Paul's instruction was designed to solidify and strengthen people's relationships. So what we take to heart as individuals we need to remember was meant for us in community also. We don't live out the truth of God's Word primarily by ourselves but almost always with others. This process, we are learning, requires a healthy understanding of forgiveness and a willingness to practice total, immediate, unilateral forgiveness.

SCRIPTURE

[32] Be kind to one another, tenderhearted, forgiving one another, as God in Christ forgave you. – Ephesians 4:32

[9] Let love be genuine. Abhor what is evil; hold fast to what is good. [10] Love one another with brotherly affection. Outdo one another in showing honor. [11] Do not be slothful in zeal, be fervent in spirit, serve the Lord. [12] Rejoice in hope, be patient in tribulation, be constant in prayer. [13] Contribute to the needs of the saints and seek to show hospitality.
[14] Bless those who persecute you; bless and do not curse them. [15] Rejoice with those who rejoice, weep with those who weep. [16] Live in harmony with one another. Do not be haughty, but associate with the lowly. Never be wise in your own sight. [17] Repay no one evil for evil, but give thought to do what is honorable in the sight of all. [18] If possible, so far as it depends on you, live peaceably with all. [19] Beloved, never avenge yourselves, but leave it to the wrath of God, for it is written, "Vengeance is mine, I will repay, says the Lord."
[20] To the contrary, "if your enemy is hungry, feed him; if he is thirsty, give him something to drink; for by so doing you will heap burning coals on his head." [21] Do not be overcome by evil, but overcome evil with good. – Romans 12:9-21

[25] I, I am he who blots out your transgressions for my own sake, and I will not remember your sins. – Isaiah 43:25

SMALL-GROUP QUESTIONS

Over the next few pages you'll find discussion questions, material that may be used as additional discussion points, and a journal exercise for group members to complete away from the group.

"As you forgive, negative, damaging emotions drain out and energy for healing is available."

1. Like a short in an electrical system or a blockage in a pipe, the expanding clog of negative emotions that develops from unforgiveness prevents relationships from functioning normally and saps energy away from other beneficial efforts. How does forgiveness affect this mess?

"When your actions change, your feelings will change."

2. What are some practical, doable examples of being kind to someone you have just forgiven?

ON THE SIDE

It seems that the last few years have seen a rise in random acts of kindness and senseless acts of beauty. There's something powerful and captivating about practicing unexpected generosity toward strangers. But there is something even more powerful about deliberate acts of kindness to people we might be tempted to describe as the last people deserving anything from us.

In the novel *Pride and Prejudice* by Jane Austen, the central figures, Elizabeth and Darcy, struggle to understand one another, which creates more harm than good. The story turns on the kindnesses that Darcy anonymously arranges for people Elizabeth loves because he has forgiven her rejection of his awkward expression of love. These two people have hurt each other, but one's efforts to practice intentional acts of kindness eventually win the heart of the other.

The challenge in practicing kindness is to be content from the outset about never being recognized for the effort. Kindness with the expectation of a payoff of some kind is calculating. Even intentional kindness should appear random.

"God forgets nothing; He doesn't forget your sin. He treats you as though it never happened."

3. How does God's refusal to throw your sins in your face motivate you to live more consistently for Him?

4. How many examples of kindness and tenderheartedness can you identify in Romans 12:9-21?

FIRSTHAND

There is probably some unforgiveness you want to drop like a hot potato now that you realize how harmful it has been for you. On the other hand, you may feel as though some unforgiveness has been superglued to you and is permanently welded to your soul. The command to forgive is not about suddenly feeling different; it is about willingly and deliberately releasing someone from the obligation that resulted when they injured you. Like a necessary surgery, it hurts now, but it will hurt much more if you don't go through with it.

There is such freedom, release, and peace waiting for us when we are no longer investing huge amounts of energy in keeping unforgiveness alive. God doesn't need our help in tracking injustice, unfairness, and wickedness. He has promised to take care of things. When we insist on hanging on to those things, we can become obstacles to God resolving difficult situations.

The testimony of those who have faced the crisis of forgiveness and entered the process will tell you unanimously that they are far better off than they were when mired in unforgiveness and the downward spiral of self-destructive emotions. This process leads to health and a closer walk with Christ, our perfect example of forgiveness.

"Attitudes are patterns of thinking formed over a long period of time."

5. What do you think people should conclude about people who claim to follow Jesus yet refuse to forgive as He did? How does unforgiveness affect the Christian witness to the world?

6. How would you explain to Jesus what you have decided to do with the forgiveness card you filled out during these sessions? Take time now to do so in prayer, asking Him for the courage and strength to follow through.

JOURNAL

This journaling opportunity is designed for group members to utilize at another time. They may choose to answer the questions in the space provided or they may prefer to use the space and time to take a deep question or concern to God.

In the first days following the crisis when you buried your forgiveness card, begin the serious process of retraining your mind to think as a forgiving person. What are the challenge points?

How are you experiencing God's Spirit at work?

YOU'RE UP

As you participate in the crisis and process of forgiveness this week, keep the following points in mind:

- Take time to thank God for the experience you've had these last few weeks. This may well be a major turning point in your life.

- Ask someone in the group to hold you accountable for developing a new pattern of thinking about forgiveness. Give him or her permission to ask you certain questions occasionally that will keep you on track.

- Stay connected with your small group. Explore what it will take to overcome the "many minor and several major" forgivenesses you will have to give as part of a local church.

- Get out the calendar you refer to most often. Flip to a date six months from now and write this question: How am I doing in the process of forgiveness?

May God bless you as you live in His grace and bless His church through your commitment to lay your unforgiveness to rest.

Leader: The following information will guide you in conducting a memorable ceremony as you Have the Funeral with your group.

As you will notice in the videos, an actual casket was used during James' messages. The final action in this study will be to write down on cards the offenders and the offenses, and then make the choice to forgive. Group members will place those cards in a "casket" for burial at the end of Session 6. This is a powerful way to drive home the truth that forgiveness has to be done, not just understood, in order for us to move forward with a healthy life.

The Card: You have permission to make copies of the card on the facing page for each member of your group—or you can design your own. These cards should be available at the first meeting of your study as James will be explaining how they are used. Group members will be preparing their cards throughout the six-week study in preparation for the funeral at the end.

The Funeral: You may plan your own ceremony (as simple or elaborate as you'd like) to be held at the end of Session 6 or perhaps the following week. The important thing is to involve your small group in a memorable, hands-on time of commitment that will forever change the way they process forgiveness.

Bonus: On the companion DVD is a bonus segment from James' church that will allow you to see and participate in the funeral service held at Harvest Bible Chapel. It would be great to view this segment with your group before the end of Session 6.

Words and music for "Good and Faithful Friend" by Andi Rozier. *www.andirozier.com.*
© Copyright 2006 Harvest Songs. All rights reserved. Used by permission.

MY FORGIVENESS CARD

Example: I forgive _____(the person)_____ for _____(the pain)_____.

I forgive _____ for _____.

I forgive _____ for _____.

I forgive _____ for _____.

I forgive _____ for _____.

I forgive _____ for _____.

I forgive _____ for _____.

I forgive _____ for _____.

I forgive _____ for _____.

I forgive _____ for _____.

I forgive _____ for _____.

I forgive _____ for _____.

Looking for your next study?
Try one of these from the Platform Series . . .